The Storm

A playscript
adapted from a story by
Roderick Hunt

by Jacquie Buttriss and Ann Callander

Characters

Narrator

Biff

Chip

Wilf

This play has four speaking parts so that it can be read aloud in small groups. Sound effects can be added by children when they are familiar with the playscript but they have not been written in.

Narrator Wilf and Wilma came to play.

Chip Come and play.

Narrator The children went outside.
They climbed the tree.

Wilf Look in the tree house.

Biff What a mess!

Narrator Dad helped the children.

Chip Mend the roof, Dad.

Biff We can mend the door.

Wilf I can paint the door.

Chip I can paint the walls.

Wilf The tree house looks good.

Biff We can put things inside.

Chip We can have a party.

Biff It's bedtime.

Narrator Biff was in her room.
She looked outside.

Biff There is a storm.

Chip It's time for school.

Narrator Wilf and Wilma came.

Wilf What a storm!

Narrator The wind blew.
The rain came down.

Biff What a storm!

Chip It's time to go home.

Biff The mums and dads are here.

Wilf What a wind!

Biff Oh no!

Wilf The tree is down.

Chip What a mess!

Biff We can climb on the tree.

Wilf Look at Floppy.

Biff Floppy has found something.

Chip It's a box.

Narrator Everyone looked at the box.

Biff Open it, Mum.

Wilf There is a key inside.

Chip I want the box.

Narrator Chip put it in his room.

The end

Printed in China by Imago